INTRODUCTION

CW00996766

Ness Battery played a vital role in the defence of the western approaches to Scapa Flow, the main fleet base for the Royal Navy in both World Wars. It is one of the best-preserved wartime sites in Britain and is the only coast battery to have retained the wooden huts of its wartime accommodation camp. One of these huts contains a remarkable example of wartime art - a painted mural depicting rural England. After an extensive programme of stabilisation and renovation, Ness Battery opened its doors to the public for the first time in 2012. This book provides a brief history of Ness Battery and a guide to these important wartime remains.

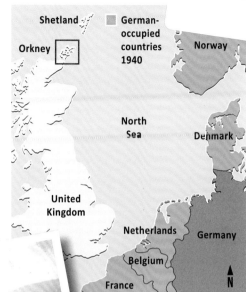

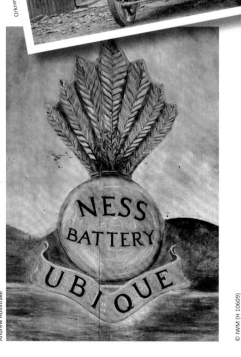

Andrew Hollinrake

© IWM (H 10609)

Orkney Library and Archive

EARLY DEFENCES OF SCAPA FLOW

Scapa Flow is one of the world's finest natural harbours. Its value as a safe haven has been recognised for centuries, and the Vikings are known to have assembled fleets of longships here. The hills of Hoy shelter the Flow from westerly gales, while entrances to the east, south and west allow sailing ships to exit or enter whatever the wind direction.

Hackness Martello Tower and Battery

Crockness Martello Tower

64-pounder gun on Hackness Martello Tower

Iain Ashman

The first significant shore-based defences of Scapa Flow came in the early 19th century with the building of Hackness Battery and the two Martello towers at Longhope in Hoy. During the Napoleonic Wars, trade with the Baltic and Scandinavian states was vital, providing Britain with essential shipbuilding materials. Convoys of as many as 100 ships would gather at Longhope under the protection of the guns, awaiting ships of the Royal Navy to escort them across the North Sea.

After decades of peace with France a new threat of war emerged. In the 1860s, new batteries were built to defend Scapa Flow, including one near the Point of Ness, manned by the Orkney Artillery Volunteers.

A new war with France never materialised, and from the 1890s the growth of Germany as a major naval power became the main threat to Britain and her Empire. As the focus moved north, Scapa Flow was to become famous throughout the world as a base for the Royal Navy.

32-pounder gun at Citadel above Stromness, no longer in use after being replaced at the Point of Ness by a 4.7-inch gun

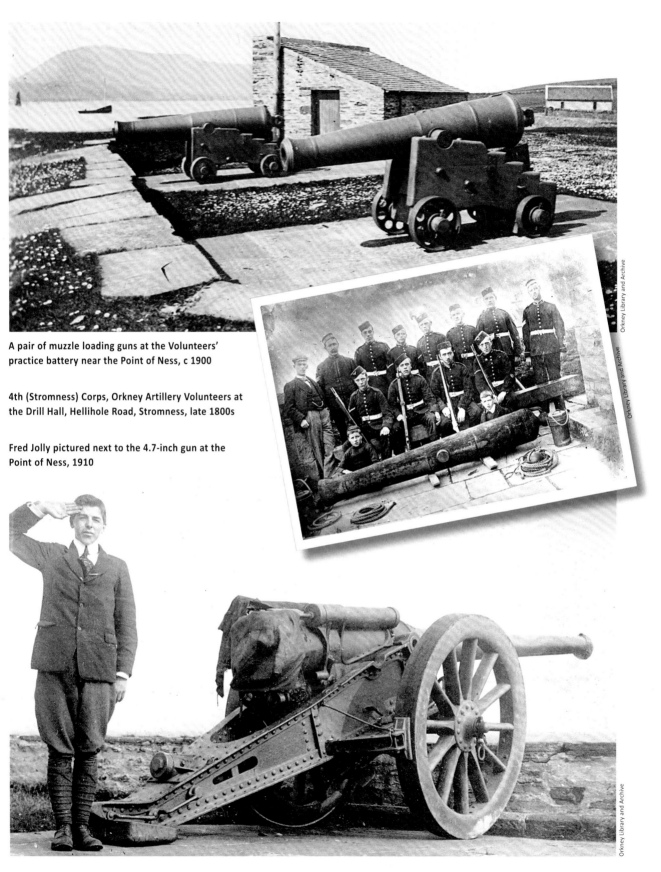

A pair of muzzle loading guns at the Volunteers' practice battery near the Point of Ness, c 1900

4th (Stromness) Corps, Orkney Artillery Volunteers at the Drill Hall, Hellihole Road, Stromness, late 1800s

Fred Jolly pictured next to the 4.7-inch gun at the Point of Ness, 1910

FIRST WORLD WAR

Orkney Library and Archive

Orkney Royal Garrison Artillery, Stromness Detachment, c 1910

In the early 1900s there was much debate about the location of a northern base for the Royal Navy. The strategic importance of Scapa Flow had been recognised, not just as an anchorage safe from attack, but also as a point from which the North Sea could be guarded. Scapa Flow was well placed to be 'the stopper in the North Sea bottle'.

By the outbreak of war on 4 August 1914, almost nothing had been done to improve the defences of Scapa Flow. Nonetheless, it was chosen as the Navy's main base, and just days before war was declared, the Grand Fleet sailed in through Hoxa Sound.

Very quickly the Navy set about defending the anchorage. Four 12-pounder guns were landed to protect Hoy Sound. Although a guard ship carrying 6-inch guns was anchored near Graemsay, the defence was considered too light and in early 1915, new guns manufactured by the Bethlehem Steel Company of Pennsylvania arrived to replace the 12-pounders. Seven of these American-made guns were shared between three new batteries built on the Stromness side of Hoy Sound. The batteries were named Hoy Nos. 1-3, numbered from west to east.

STROMNESS

N

Hoy No. 1
Two 6-inch guns

Hoy No. 2
Two 6-inch guns

Hoy No. 3
Three 5-inch guns

Pre-WWI
Volunteers'
Battery

Two
12-pounder
guns

Two
12-pounder
guns

0 Kilometre   1

0 Mile   1

Remains of
Hoy No. 3 Battery

The remains of some elements of Hoy No. 2 Battery can still be seen amongst the WWII structures of Ness Battery. The WWI emplacements were of the 'open barbette' type, with no overhead cover since there was little or no threat from air attack. The emplacements had low parapet walls and ammunition lockers to keep a small amount of shells at hand, while the main supply was kept in magazines to the rear.

Orkney's coast batteries were not called upon to fire in anger during WWI, since Germany never attempted an attack on Scapa Flow with surface vessels. But the guns would have been fired for practice on a regular basis. One of the guns at Hoy No. 3 was used to support the Navy's Examination Service which controlled traffic in and out of Hoy Sound, and would have fired a shot across the bows of a vessel when required. This role was to be repeated at Ness Battery during WWII.

Orkney Library and Archive

Hoy No. 1 Battery, showing the Battery Observation Post (left), the accommodation huts (right) and what are probably the cowled ventilation shafts for a magazine in the foreground. The concrete gun emplacements are just out of view to the left.

American-built 5-inch gun, Hoy Battery No. 3

Orkney Library and Archive

Iain Ashman

5

BETWEEN THE WARS

The signing of the Armistice in November 1918 brought an end to hostilities, but a state of war still existed until the signing of the Treaty of Versailles in June 1919. One of the conditions of the Armistice was the internment of the ships of the German High Seas Fleet. The Allies failed to find a neutral port willing to take on the role, so Scapa Flow was chosen to hold the German ships. Rear Admiral von Reuter, the commanding officer, suspected that once the Treaty was signed, he would have to hand over control of his ships to the Allies. To prevent this final humiliation, he ordered the scuttling of the ships on 21 June 1919. Until then, Orkney's coast batteries had a role to play in preventing the escape of the German ships, particularly while the Royal Navy's ships were out on manoeuvres.

Scapa Flow did not revert to the status of a peacetime base until 1920, but by the end of that year the dismantling of the defences of Scapa Flow was well underway, including the coast batteries. The guns at Hoy No. 2 (Ness) were among the last to go, sold in late 1920 to James Sutherland, the Stromness coal merchant, for £1 apiece. In 1922, Sutherland used explosives to break up the guns then sold the metal for scrap. The wooden huts of the battery's camp were sold off the same year.

SMS *Bayern* sinking by the stern

SMS *Hindenburg*

Orkney Library and Archive

Orkney Library and Archive

Interned German High Seas Fleet, Scapa Flow, 28 May 1919

A 6-inch Mark VII gun in Iceland. This shows how the temporary emplacements at Ness Battery would have looked in 1938.

The Navy continued to use the anchorage between the wars, with frequent visits made by the Atlantic Fleet (later renamed the Home Fleet) throughout the 1920s and 30s. Meanwhile, most of the German ships were raised from the seabed, towed south and cut up for scrap.

Soon after Adolf Hitler became Chancellor in 1933, Germany withdrew from the League of Nations and began rearming in earnest. In 1936, German forces reoccupied the Rhineland in violation of the Treaty of Versailles, and by 1938 Hitler was threatening to invade Czechoslovakia. Britain had begun to rearm, reluctantly, in response to Germany's aggression.

Rosyth on the Firth of Forth had initially been chosen as the main base for the Home Fleet in the event of war, with Scapa Flow as a secondary base. Early in 1938, a unit of Territorial Army gunners was raised in Orkney to man a new anti-aircraft battery at Lyness in Hoy, where a new fuel depot was being built. Later that year, as war with Germany looked more and more likely, guns were put in place to guard the main entrances to Scapa Flow. Two pairs of 6-inch guns were installed; one pair at Stanger

Head in Flotta to cover Hoxa Sound, the other pair at Ness Battery, covering Hoy Sound. The Ness guns were in place on temporary mountings by the end of July 1938.

The immediate threat of war receded with the signing of the Munich Agreement in September 1938. Despite Prime Minister Neville Chamberlain's assurances of 'peace for our time', Britain continued to rearm. In Orkney, two new Territorial units were raised to man the coast batteries. The Orkney Heavy Regiment, Royal Artillery (TA) manned the guns, while the Orkney Fortress Company, Royal Engineers (TA) operated the engine rooms and searchlights.

In January 1939 it was confirmed that Scapa Flow, not Rosyth, would be the main base for the Home Fleet. In late August, the Orkney TA units were mobilised and sent to their war stations. When war was declared on 3 September, work was still underway on the gun emplacements, magazines and wooden huts at Ness. The searchlights were still only housed in corrugated-iron shelters, the guns still on their temporary mountings, but Ness Battery was manned and ready to defend Scapa Flow.

SECOND WORLD WAR

As the Orkney Territorials stood ready at Ness Battery's guns, work continued on the concrete structures and wooden accommodation huts. In the first few weeks of the war, German reconnaissance planes were frequently sighted over Scapa Flow, air raid warnings sounded and on a few occasions, the 6-inch guns at Ness were used to fire 'bring-to' rounds across the bows of suspect vessels trying to enter Hoy Sound, one of which was later identified as a Royal Navy store ship.

A unit of the Royal Navy's Examination Service was based at Ness to control traffic through Hoy Sound, with Ness becoming the Examination Battery. Although most of the Royal Navy's ships used Hoxa Sound to enter Scapa Flow, Hoy Sound was always busy, with Stromness the main harbour into which Army troops, supplies, food, coal and ammunition were brought.

The sinking of HMS *Royal Oak* in the early hours of 14 October 1939 by the German submarine *U-47* made it all too clear that the anchorage was not safe. HMS *Iron Duke* was crippled and almost sunk by air attack a few days later, and the ships of the Home Fleet were dispersed to other Naval anchorages around Scotland. In response, new plans were drawn up to improve the defences of Scapa Flow.

HMS *Royal Oak*

Orkney Library and Archive

to their aircraft the Luftwaffe's attacks became few and far between.

Meanwhile, Ness Battery was nearing completion. The guns had been moved into their permanent emplacements, the underground magazines were ready with powered ammunition lifts, and a Battery Observation Post was being built to replace the temporary structure just behind the guns. Further huts were added to the camp as it expanded to accommodate the extra personnel of the Fire Command, Examination Service and Regimental Headquarters.

Ness Battery was kept busy supporting the Examination Service throughout the war. In August 1940, a round had to be fired across the bows of the mail boat, *St Ola*, to prevent her entering the harbour. Hoy Sound had been closed to all vessels after a German plane had been seen dropping parachute mines. The Master of the *St Ola*, Captain Swanson, had not been informed before he left Scrabster, and in very rough weather may not have seen the signal from Ness Battery as he approached. Disaster was averted, and the *St Ola* returned to Scrabster, although most of her passengers were 'about half dead from sickness'.

St Ola

Image courtesy of Bruce Gorie

By early March 1940, Scapa Flow was deemed safe enough for the Home Fleet to return. Around that time, air raids intensified, with German bombers targeting the Navy's ships. By now, the anti-aircraft cover - known as the 'Scapa Barrage' - was very effective, and in the face of heavy losses

The Orkney coast batteries were not called upon to fire in anger throughout WWII. As in WWI, Germany never attacked Scapa Flow with surface vessels, a tribute perhaps to the deterrent effect of such a concentration of firepower around the entrances to Scapa Flow.

Bofors anti-aircraft gun overlooking Ness Battery, 1944

© IWM (H 33453)

Links Battery

Searchlight emplacement

MAINLAND

Ness Battery

Stromness

Links Battery

Hoy Mouth

Blockships

Graemsay Battery

GRAEMSAY

Skerry Battery

Burra Sound

Controlled minefield

Houton Battery

HOY

Bring Deeps

Hoy Sound in WWII, showing the six batteries of Stromness Fire Command

Scad Battery

Boom defence and anti-submarine nets

| 0 Kilometre | 2 |
| 0 Mile | 2 |

ORKNEY

Scapa Flow

N

N

Ness Battery

RAF aerial photo taken in 1946

Orkney Sites and Monuments Record

Ness Battery Observation Post, 1941

Andrew Hollinrake

Battery Observation Post and Fire Command

This imposing building was the nerve centre of Ness Battery, and from here the seaward defences of Hoy Sound were co-ordinated.

The Battery Observation Post (BOP), to the left of the complex of buildings when viewed from the front, housed the rangefinder. This could very simply and quickly be used to calculate the range of a target by measuring the downward angle from its known, fixed height. The information was then passed on to the gun emplacements via cables to dials below the guns. Above the BOP was the Searchlight Directing Station, a small compartment from which the two searchlights down by the shore were remotely controlled.

The Fire Command was housed in the bottom right corner of the complex. From here the fire of all six batteries of 534 Coast Regiment could be co-ordinated. On the ground floor, a large plotting table with a gridded map showing the batteries and their arcs of fire was used to plot targets.

Later in the war Ness Battery was equipped with radar, mounted on the roof of the Fire Command building. This could be used to provide range and bearing information on targets, and could detect the splash created by the fall-of-shot when shells missed their target. This data could then be relayed to the BOP of the relevant battery, and appropriate corrections made before the next salvo.

At the top right of the building was the Port War Signal Station (PWSS). From here, the Navy maintained control of all shipping going in and out of Hoy Sound. The Examination Vessel, usually a converted fishing boat or 'drifter', patrolled the harbour entrance, keeping in touch with the PWSS by signal lamp. Most incoming traffic was authorised in advance, so if expected and showing the correct coded signals, vessels would be allowed to proceed.

Searchlight Directing Station　　　　　　Port War Signal Station

Battery Observation Post　　　　Fire Command

Andrew Hollinrake

Ness Battery today

Battery Observation Post

Andrew Hollinrake

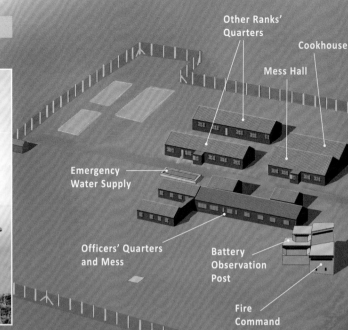

Other Ranks' Quarters

Cookhouse

Mess Hall

Emergency Water Supply

Officers' Quarters and Mess

Battery Observation Post

Fire Command

Latrine Block

Engine Room

Andrew Hollinrake

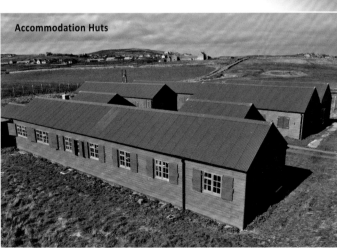

Accommodation Huts

Andrew Hollinrake

No. 2 Emplacement

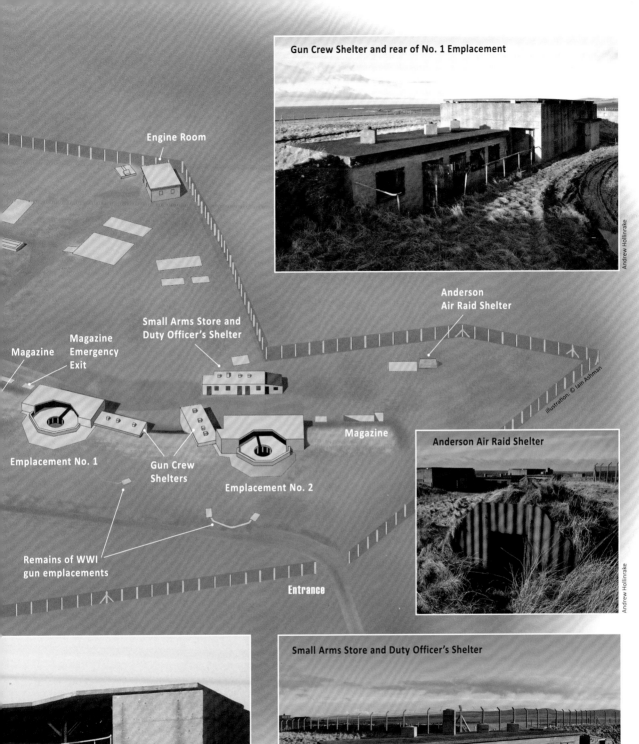

Gun Crew Shelter and rear of No. 1 Emplacement

Andrew Hollinrake

Engine Room

Anderson
Air Raid Shelter

Small Arms Store and
Duty Officer's Shelter

Magazine
Emergency
Exit

Magazine

Illustration, © Iain Ashman

Emplacement No. 1

Gun Crew
Shelters

Magazine

Emplacement No. 2

Remains of WWI
gun emplacements

Entrance

Anderson Air Raid Shelter

Andrew Hollinrake

Tom Ashman

Small Arms Store and Duty Officer's Shelter

Andrew Hollinrake

The Gun Emplacements

At the front of the battery, facing out to sea, stand the two concrete gun emplacements which housed the 6-inch calibre guns.

Circular concrete platforms surround the gun pits in which the guns were fixed on tall mountings. Each mounting was fixed to a holdfast, a ring of bolts set deep into the concrete. Around the back of the platform are lockers for a small amount of 'ready-use' ammunition. The overhead cover protected the gun crews from aerial attack. The nine-man crew operated the gun from the raised platform. The 'No. 1' was in command, issuing orders for loading and firing, while three men on the optical sights aimed the gun at the target. The rest of the crew loaded the gun and operated the breech.

These photographs, taken in June 1941, show how the emplacements were camouflaged before the overhead canopies were added. Local stone was built up over the bare concrete to create the appearance of ruined farm buildings. The Reserve Watch (above) pass shells and cartridges to the Duty Watch, who operate the gun as an officer looks on (below).

The duty gun crew spent most of their watch in a shelter attached to the side of the emplacement, but at least one of the men remained on lookout by the gun at all times. The off-duty crew, or

Reserve Watch, would be back at the camp, kept in a state of readiness. They would come up to the gun position when the alarm was sounded, to man the magazine and keep the gun crew supplied with ammunition.

The 6-inch Mark VII gun had been designed as a naval weapon in 1898. Its long, slender barrel produced a high muzzle velocity, ideal for penetrating the armour of ships. It fired a 6-inch (152mm) diameter shell weighing 100lbs (45kg), propelled through the barrel by the cartridge, a silk bag of cordite explosive. The shell was placed in the breech and rammed home, then the cartridge was loaded behind it. The breech was then closed and the gun was ready to fire. The guns had a range of just over seven miles (11km). A well-trained crew could load and fire up to eight rounds-per-minute, and at maximum range it was possible to fire the fourth round before the first shell had hit the water.

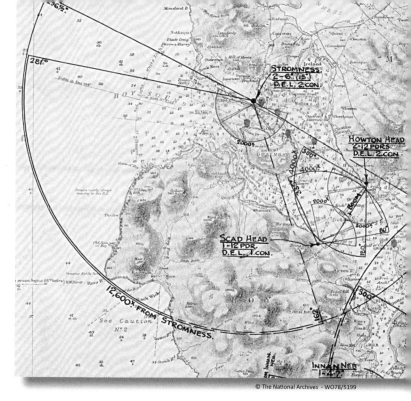

An early 1940 plan showing the arcs of fire and searchlight coverage for Ness, Houton and Scad Batteries. This plan was made before Links, Skerry and Graemsay Batteries were established, and at this point Ness was still known as Stromness Battery.

Night gunnery practice, 1941

No. 1 Emplacement, 1944

© IWM (H 39434)

© IWM (H 39432)

By the end of 1941, the concrete shelters were complete, with overhead cover to protect the gun crews from aerial attack. The gunlayers operated the sights within a splinter shield surrounding the breech of the gun.

No. 1 Emplacement

Battery Observation Post

No. 2 gun during practice, 1944. A shell is being loaded at the breech, while the 'No. 4' is poised to ram the shell home.

No. 2 Emplacement

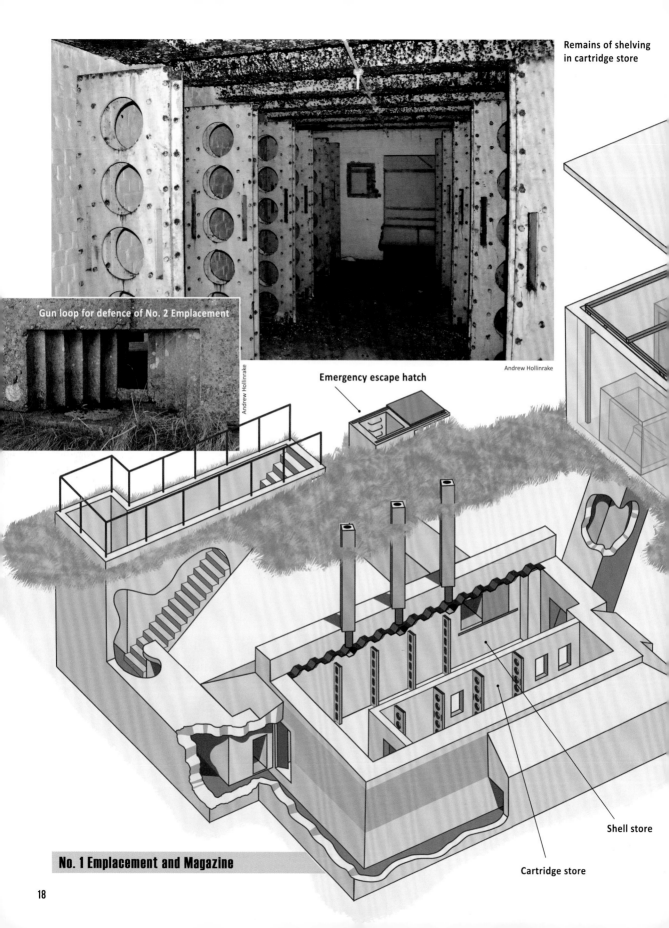

Remains of shelving in cartridge store

Gun loop for defence of No. 2 Emplacement

Andrew Hollinrake

Andrew Hollinrake

Emergency escape hatch

Shell store

Cartridge store

No. 1 Emplacement and Magazine

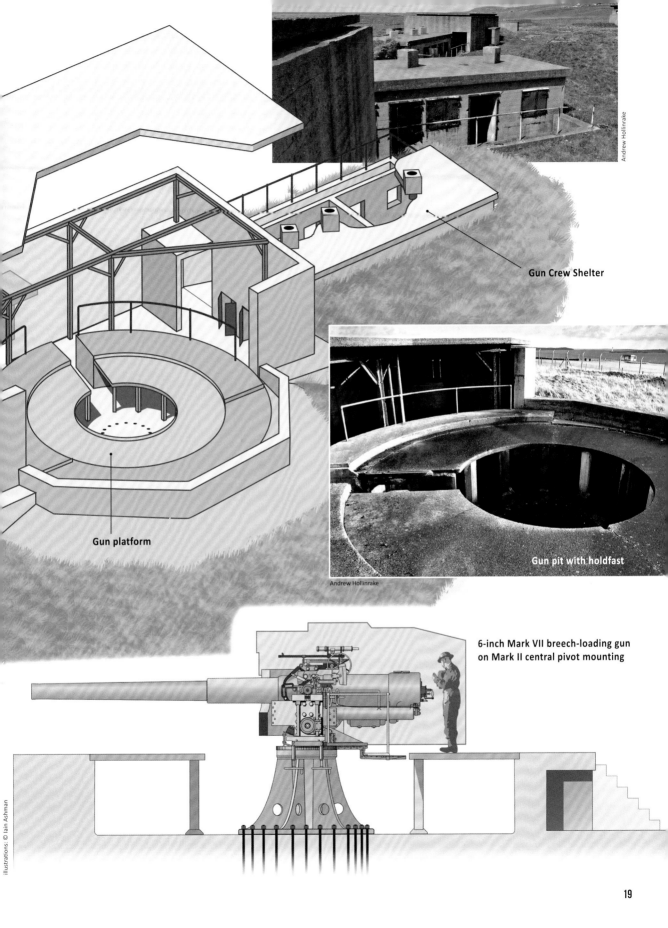

Andrew Hollinrake

Gun Crew Shelter

Gun platform

Gun pit with holdfast

Andrew Hollinrake

6-inch Mark VII breech-loading gun
on Mark II central pivot mounting

illustrations: © Iain Ashman

The Magazines

A small amount of ammunition was kept in the 'ready-use' lockers around the rear of each gun emplacement, but the bulk was kept in underground magazines. Each magazine had two large chambers, one for storing shells, the other for cartridges. A powered conveyor belt carried the ammunition up to the gun shelter.

The entrance to each magazine was down a narrow flight of concrete steps, descending to 25ft (8m) below ground level. The ammunition was lowered down by a small crane mounted on the concrete. Heavily-armoured ceilings and steel doors protected the chambers from bomb blast.

© IWM (TR 571)

In a magazine at a WWII coast battery in Dover, Kent, a gunner carefully extracts a cartridge. It will be taken to the gun in the flash-proof 'Clarkson's Case'.

Setting fuzes on 6-inch high-explosive shells in a coast battery magazine

Remains of shelving in shell store, Ness Battery

© IWM (H 12958)

Andrew Hollinrake

The Searchlights

For firing at night, two searchlights were installed by the shore below Ness Battery. Known as fighting lights, they each sent out a concentrated movable beam, like giant spotlights searching Hoy Sound for enemy ships. These were powerful carbon-arc lamps, 15kW each, requiring a huge amount of electricity. The main generators were housed in the Engine Room, well behind the gun emplacements, with a single back-up generator in a small concrete building just behind the searchlights.

The lights were operated from the Searchlight Directing Station by remote control, exposing or dousing the lights and changing the elevation and bearing. A small maintenance crew in the searchlight emplacement kept the light burning, and could operate the light manually if the control cables were cut.

Gunner E A Leggett from Woking, Surrey, cleans the front of a 90cm searchlight in its emplacement near Links Battery. Of the six searchlight emplacements which served Links and Ness Batteries, only this one remains.

The Camp

Ness is believed to be the only coast battery in Britain to have retained the wooden huts of its wartime accommodation camp. This gives us a unique insight into the daily lives of the men stationed here.

The largest of the blocks was for the officers. In the Officers' Mess they could relax by an open fire, smoke and have a drink. Along the corridor were the sleeping quarters, each room with its own coal-fired stove. At either end of the main building were the kitchen and bathroom blocks. Some of the original fittings survive, including a cast-iron bath.

Two of the four huts built for accommodating the Other Ranks remain. These were far more crowded than the Sergeants' and Officers' sleeping quarters with up to 32 men in each hut. Each had a single stove in the centre with rows of bunk beds along both sides. There were wash basins and toilets in the huts but the main shower blocks and latrines were outside in draughty Nissen huts. Next to the Other Ranks' huts stand the Cookhouse and Mess Hall. Up to 120 men could be fed at one sitting, and there was always a hot drink available for men coming off watch.

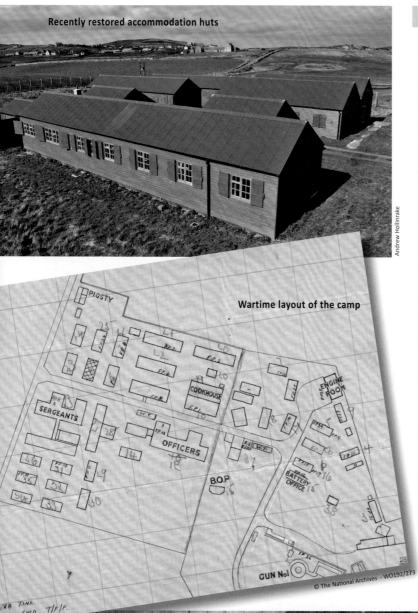

Recently restored accommodation huts

Andrew Hollinrake

Wartime layout of the camp

© The National Archives - WO192/273

Part of the Mess Hall mural

Andrew Hollinrake/ORCA

The Mess Hall is of particular interest due to the painted mural which covers most of the walls inside. It depicts scenes of rural England including a thatched cottage, a gypsy camp, a village pub and a windmill perched on a hill. The artist signed his name, AR Woods, and it is thought that the man in question was Albert Rycraft Woods, a piermaster who worked for the Port of London Authority.

Andrew Hollinrake

Albert's memoirs, *I Guarded The Waterfront*, were published in 1942, and although he makes no mention of Orkney, there is plenty of information in the book which fits with detail in the mural. For example, he grew up in Gravesend, Kent, and the windmill in the painting resembles very closely one which used to overlook the town. The mural also depicts oast houses, rarely seen outside Kent.

If this is the same man, he would have been in his sixties during WWII, so it seems unlikely that he was on active service. He may have come to the islands with equipment such as floating cranes, tenders and barges, supplied by the Port of London Authority for naval use in Scapa Flow. Whatever the reason for his presence in Orkney, he must have been at Ness Battery for some time - long enough to paint the remarkable mural.

Soldiers from around Britain were brought in to swell the ranks, both at Ness and other batteries. Although Orkney counted as an overseas posting, entitling the soldiers to a higher rate of pay and longer periods of leave, it was not a popular destination. Many of the gunners had been transferred from the defences of the south coast of England, and they would have found the Orkney winters particularly harsh. The scenery of the mural would have been a warm and comforting image of home for them, perhaps even a reminder of what they were fighting for.

Albert Rycraft Woods pictured on Tower Pier, with his dog Peter

In 2012, conservators worked on cleaning and restoring the painted mural. In one area, the discoloured varnish was stripped away to reveal the vibrant colours hidden underneath.

Authors' collection

1945 TO THE PRESENT DAY

6-inch gun after WWII, with breech removed and sealed

Practice on a mobile 3.7-inch gun at Ness Battery, c 1953

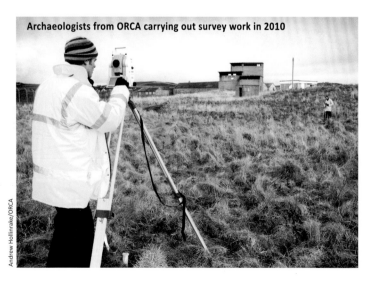

Archaeologists from ORCA carrying out survey work in 2010

Ness Battery remained operational until June 1945, when the 6-inch guns were put into 'Care and Maintenance'. In 1950 they were put back into action for practice by the Orkney Territorial Army, and the battery became known as 'No. 49 WETC' (Weekend Training Centre). In 1955, the guns and searchlights were returned to the Royal Arsenal at Woolwich.

The Orkney TA, as well as regular Army units, continued to use Ness Battery for training until the 1990s. Local Army and Sea Cadets were regular visitors, as were school and cadet groups from the UK mainland. The Northern Lighthouse Board built a helipad at Ness Battery in the early 1970s to supply the lighthouses around the north of Scotland.

The Ministry of Defence sold the site to Orkney Islands Council in 2001. In 2009 a programme of research, restoration and stabilisation was implemented by the Scapa Flow Landscape Partnership Scheme, funded by Orkney Islands Council, Historic Scotland, Heritage Lottery Fund and European Regional Development Fund.

New steel supports were installed in the gun emplacements, where the original girders had rusted almost to the point of collapse. The leaking asbestos roofs on the huts, dating from the 1970s, were removed and replaced with corrugated iron, closer to the original wartime style. Conservation work was carried out on the mural, and research continues into the history of Ness Battery. Further work is planned which will make more of the buildings safe for public access, such as the magazines and officers' quarters.

Orkney's wartime remains are now recognised as an important resource for the understanding and appreciation of Scapa Flow's vital role during the two World Wars. Ness Battery played its part in making the anchorage safe for the Royal Navy, and now that it has been preserved, this unique site is an ideal place to tell the story.